BOA
EDITIONS
LIMITED

What We Carry

POEMS BY

DORIANNE LAUX

BOA EDITIONS, LTD. • BROCKPORT, NY • 1994

Copyright © 1994 by Dorianne Laux
All rights reserved

LC #: 94–71369
ISBN: 978-1-880238-06-6 cloth
ISBN: 978-1-880238-07-3 paper

10 11 12   13 12 11

For information about permission to use any material from this book please contact
The Permissions Company at www.permissionscompany.com or e-mail permdude@eclipse.net

The publication of books by BOA Editions, Ltd.,
is made possible with the assistance of grants from
the Literature Program of the New York State Council on the Arts
and the Literature Program of the National Endowment for the Arts,
as well as from the Lannan Foundation, the Lila Wallace–Reader's Digest
Literary Publishers Marketing Development Program,
and the Rochester Area Foundation.

Cover Design: Daphne Poulin
Typesetting: R. Foerster, York Beach, ME
Manufacturing: Bookmobile
BOA Logo: Mirko

NATIONAL
ENDOWMENT
FOR THE ARTS
A great nation
deserves great art.

BOA Editions, Ltd.
250 North Goodman Street, Suite 306
Rochester, NY 14607
www.boaeditions.org
A Poulin Jr., Founder (1938-1996)

State of the Arts

NYSCA

Contents

AS IT IS / 49

for my mother

WHAT WE CARRY

Late October

Midnight. The cats under the open window,
their guttural, territorial yowls.

Crouched in the neighbor's driveway with a broom,
I jab at them with the bristle end,

chasing their raised tails as they scramble
from bush to bush, intent on killing each other.

I shout and kick until they finally
give it up; one shimmies beneath the fence,

the other under a car. I stand in my underwear
in the trembling quiet, remembering my dream.

Something had been stolen from me, valueless
and irreplaceable. Grease and grass blades

were stuck to the bottoms of my feet.
I was shaking and sweating. I had wanted

to *kill* them. The moon was a white dinner plate
broken exactly in half. I saw myself as I was:

forty-one years old, standing on a slab
of cold concrete, a broom handle slipping

from my hands, my breasts bare, my hair
on end, afraid of what I might do next.

Dust

Someone spoke to me last night,
told me the truth. Just a few words,
but I recognized it.
I knew I should make myself get up,
write it down, but it was late,
and I was exhausted from working
all day in the garden, moving rocks.
Now, I remember only the flavor —
not like food, sweet or sharp.
More like a fine powder, like dust.
And I wasn't elated or frightened,
but simply rapt, aware.
That's how it is sometimes —
God comes to your window,
all bright light and black wings,
and you're just too tired to open it.

If This Is Paradise

The true mystery of the world is the visible . . .
— OSCAR WILDE

If this is paradise: trees, beehives,
boulders. And this: bald moon, shooting
stars, a little sun. If in your hands
this is paradise: sensate flesh,
hidden bone, your own eyes
opening, then why should we speak?
Why not lift into each day like the animals
that we are and go silently
about our true business: the hunt
for water, fat berries, the mushroom's
pale meat, tumble through waist-high grasses
without reason, find shade and rest there,
our limbs spread beneath the meaningless sky,
find the scent of the lover
and mate wildly. If this is paradise
and all we have to do is be born and live
and die, why pick up the stick at all?
Why see the wheel in the rock?
Why bring back from the burning fields
a bowl full of fire and pretend that it's magic?

What Could Happen

Noon. A stale Saturday. The hills
rise above the town, nudge houses and shops
toward the valley, kick the shallow river
into place. Here, a dog can bark for days

and no one will care enough
to toss an empty can or an unread newspaper
in his direction. No one complains.
The men stand in loose knots

outside Ace Hardware, talk a little, stare
at the blue tools. A few kids
sulk through the park, the sandbox full
of hardscrabble, the monkey bars

too hot to touch. In a town like this
a woman on the edge of forty
could drive around in her old car, the back end
all jingle and rivet, one headlight

taped in place, the hood held down with greasy rope,
and no one would notice.
She could drive up and down the same street
all day, eating persimmons,

stopping only for a moment to wonder
at the wooden Indian on the corner of 6th and B,
the shop window behind it
filled with beaten leather, bright woven goods

from Guatemala, postcards of this town
before it began to go under, began
to fade into a likeness of itself.
She could pull in at the corner store for a soda

and pause before uncapping it,
press the cold glass against her cheek,
roll it under her palm down the length of her neck
then slip it beneath the V of her blouse

and let it rest there, where she's hottest.
She could get back in her car
and turn the key, bring the engine up
like a swarm of bottle flies, feel it

shake like an empty caboose.
She could twist the radio too high
and drive like this for the rest of the day —
the same street, the same hairpin turn

that knocks the jack in the trunk from one wheel well
to the other — or she could pass the turn
and keep going, the cold soda
wedged between her legs, the bass notes

throbbing like a vein, out past the closed shops
and squat houses, the church
with its bland white arch, toward the hills,
beyond that shadowy nest of red madrones.

After Twelve Days of Rain

I couldn't name it, the sweet
sadness welling up in me for weeks.
So I cleaned, found myself standing
in a room with a rag in my hand,
the birds calling *time-to-go, time-to-go*.
And like an old woman near the end
of her life I could hear it, the voice
of a man I never loved who pressed
my breasts to his lips and whispered
"My little doves, my white, white lilies."
I could almost cry when I remember it.

I don't remember when I began
to call everyone "sweetie,"
as if they were my daughters,
my darlings, my little birds.
I have always loved too much,
or not enough. Last night
I read a poem about God and almost
believed it — God sipping coffee,
smoking cherry tobacco. I've arrived
at a time in my life when I could believe
almost anything.

Today, pumping gas into my old car, I stood
hatless in the rain and the whole world
went silent — cars on the wet street
sliding past without sound, the attendant's
mouth opening and closing on air
as he walked from pump to pump, his footsteps
erased in the rain — nothing
but the tiny numbers in their square windows
rolling by my shoulder, the unstoppable seconds

gliding by as I stood at the Chevron,
balanced evenly on my two feet, a gas nozzle
gripped in my hand, my hair gathering rain.

And I saw it didn't matter
who had loved me or who I loved. I was alone.
The black oily asphalt, the slick beauty
of the Iranian attendant, the thickening
clouds — nothing was mine. And I understood
finally, after a semester of philosophy,
a thousand books of poetry, after death
and childbirth and the startled cries of men
who called out my name as they entered me,
I finally believed I was alone, felt it
in my actual, visceral heart, heard it echo
like a thin bell. And the sounds
came back, the slish of tires
and footsteps, all the delicate cargo
they carried saying thank you
and yes. So I paid and climbed into my car
as if nothing had happened —
as if everything mattered — What else could I do?

I drove to the grocery store
and bought wheat bread and milk,
a candy bar wrapped in gold foil,
smiled at the teenaged cashier
with the pimpled face and the plastic
name plate pinned above her small breast,
and knew her secret, her sweet fear —
Little bird. Little darling. She handed me
my change, my brown bag, a torn receipt,
pushed the cash drawer in with her hip
and smiled back.

Aphasia

---

for Honeya

After the stroke all she could say
was *Venezuela*, pointing to the pitcher
with its bright blue rim, her one word
command. And when she drank the clear
water in and gave the glass back,
it was *Venezuela* again, gratitude,
maybe, or the word now simply
a sigh, like the sky in the window,
the pillows a cloudy definition
propped beneath her head. Pink roses
dying on the bedside table, each fallen
petal a scrap in the shape of a country
she'd never been to, had never once
expressed interest in, and now
it was everywhere, in the peach
she lifted, dripping, to her lips,
the white tissue in the box, her brooding
children when they came to visit,
baptized with their new name
after each kiss. And at night
she whispered it, dark narcotic
in her husband's ear as he bent
to listen, her hands fumbling
at her buttons, her breasts,
holding them up to the light
like a gift. *Venezuela*, she said.

Graveyard at Hurd's Gulch

His grave is strewn with litter again,
crumpled napkins, a plastic spoon, white
styrofoam cup tipped on its side, bright
half-moon of lipstick on the rim.
I want to scold her for the mess she's left,
the flattened grass and squashed grapes,
but I've seen her walking toward the trees,
her hollow body receding, her shadow
following behind. I'm the intruder,
come not to mourn a specific body
but to rest under a tree, my finger tracing
the rows of glowing marble,
the cloud-covered hips of the hills.
I always take the same spot,
next to the sunken stone that says MOTHER,
the carved dates with the little dash between them,
a brief, deep cut, like a metaphor for life.
Does she whisper, I wonder, to the one
she loves, or simply eat and sleep, content
for an hour above the bed of his bones?
I think she brings him oranges and secrets,
her day's torn and intricate lace.
I have no one on this hill to dine with.
I'm blessed. Everyone I love is still alive.
I know there is no God, no afterlife,
but there is this peace, the granite angel
with moss-covered wings whose face
I have grown to love, her sad smile
like that sadness we feel after sex,
those few delirious hours when we needed nothing
but breath and flesh, after we've flown back
into ourselves, our imperfect heavy bodies,
just before the terrible hunger returns.

What We Carry

for Donald

He tells me his mother carries his father's ashes
on the front seat in a cardboard box, exactly
where she placed them after the funeral.
Her explanation: she hasn't decided
where they should be scattered.
It's been three years.
I imagine her driving home from the store,
a sack of groceries jostling next to the box —
smell of lemons, breakfast rolls,
the radio tuned to the news.
He says he never liked his father,
but made peace with him before he died.
That he carries what he can
and discards the rest.
We are sitting in a cafe.
Because I don't love him, I love
to watch him watch the women walk by
in their sheer summer skirts.
From where I sit I can see them approach,
then study his face as he watches them go.
We are friends. We are both lonely.
I never tell him about my father
so he doesn't know that when I think of his —
blue ashes in a cardboard box — I think
of my own, alive in a room
somewhere in Oregon, a woman
helping his worn body into bed, the same body
that crushed my sister's childhood, mine.
Maybe this wife kisses him
goodnight, tells him she loves him,
actually means it. This close to the end,

if he asked forgiveness, what could I say?
If I were handed my father's ashes,
what would I do with them?
What body of water would be fit
for his scattering? What ground?
It's best when I think least. I listen
to my friend's story without judgement
or surprise, taking it in as he takes in
the women, without question, simply a given,
as unexceptional as conversation between friends,
the laughter and at each end
the relative comfort of silence.

The Job

for Tobey

When my friend lost her little finger
between the rollers of a printing press,
I hadn't met her yet. It must have taken
months for the stump to heal, skin stretched
and stitched over bone, must have taken
years before she could consider it calmly,
as she does now, in an airport cafe
over a cup of black coffee.
She doesn't complain or blame the unguarded
machine, the noise of the factory, the job
with its long unbroken hours.
She simply opens her damaged hand and studies
the emptiness, the loss
of symmetry and flesh, and tells me
it was a small price to pay,
that her missing finger taught her
to take more care with her life,
with what she reaches out
to touch, to stay awake when she's awake
and listen, to pay attention
to what's turning in the world.

For the Sake of Strangers

No matter what the grief, its weight,
we are obliged to carry it.
We rise and gather momentum, the dull strength
that pushes us through crowds.
And then the young boy gives me directions
so avidly. A woman holds the glass door open,
waits patiently for my empty body to pass through.
All day it continues, each kindness
reaching toward another — a stranger
singing to no one as I pass on the path, trees
offering their blossoms, a retarded child
who lifts his almond eyes and smiles.
Somehow they always find me, seem even
to be waiting, determined to keep me
from myself, from the thing that calls to me
as it must have once called to them —
this temptation to step off the edge
and fall weightless, away from the world.

What I Wouldn't Do

The only job I didn't like, quit
after the first shift, was selling
subscriptions to TV Guide over the phone.
Before that it was fast food, all
the onion rings I could eat, handing
sacks of deep fried burritos through
the sliding window, the hungry hands
grabbing back. And at the laundromat,
plucking bright coins from a palm
or pressing them into one, kids
screaming from the bathroom and twenty
dryers on high. Cleaning houses was fine,
polishing the knick-knacks of the rich.
I liked holding the hand-blown glass bell
from Czechoslovakia up to the light,
the jewelled clapper swinging lazily
from side to side, its foreign,
A-minor ping. I drifted, an itinerant,
from job to job, the sanatorium
where I pureed peas and carrots
and stringy beets, scooped them,
like pudding, onto flesh-colored
plastic plates, or the gas station
where I dipped the ten-foot measuring stick
into the hole in the blacktop,
pulled it up hand over hand
into the twilight, dripping
its liquid gold, pink-tinged.
I liked the donut shop best, 3 AM,
alone in the kitchen, surrounded
by sugar and squat mounds of dough,
the flashing neon sign strung from wire
behind the window, gilding my white uniform

yellow, then blue, then drop-dead red.
It wasn't that I hated calling them, hour
after hour, stuck in a booth with a list
of strangers' names, dialing their numbers
with the eraser end of a pencil and them
saying hello. It was that moment
of expectation, before I answered back,
the sound of their held breath,
their disappointment when they realized
I wasn't who they thought I was,
the familiar voice, or the voice they loved
and had been waiting all day to hear.

Singing Back the World

I don't remember how it began.
The singing. Judy at the wheel
in the middle of *Sentimental Journey*.
The side of her face glowing.
Her full lips moving. Beyond her shoulder
the little houses sliding by.
And Geri. Her frizzy hair tumbling
in the wind wing's breeze, fumbling
with the words. All of us singing
as loud as we can. Off key.
Not even a semblance of harmony.
Driving home in a blue Comet singing
I'll Be Seeing You and *Love Is a Rose*.
The love songs of war. The war songs
of love. Mixing up verses, eras, words.
Songs from stupid musicals.
Coming in strong on the easy refrains.
Straining our middle aged voices
trying to reach impossible notes,
reconstruct forgotten phrases.
Cole Porter's *Anything Goes*.
Shamelessly la la la-ing
whole sections. Forgetting
the rent, the kids, the men,
the other woman. The sad goodbye.
The whole of childhood. Forgetting
the lost dog. Polio. The grey planes
pregnant with bombs. Fields
of white headstones. All of it gone
as we struggle to remember
the words. One of us picking up
where the others leave off. Intent
on the song. Forgetting our bodies,

their pitiful limbs, their heaviness.
Nothing but three throats
beating back the world — Laurie's
radiation treatments. The scars
on Christina's arms. Kim's brother.
Molly's grandfather. Jane's sister.
Singing to the telephone poles
skimming by. Stoplights
blooming green. The road,
a glassy black river edged
with brilliant gilded weeds. The car
an immense boat cutting the air
into blue angelic plumes. Singing
Blue Moon and *Paper Moon*
and *Mack the Knife*, and *Nobody Knows*
the Trouble I've Seen.

Balance

I'm remembering again, the day
we stood on the porch and you smoked
while the old man told you
about his basement full of wine,
his bad heart and the doctor's warning,
how he held the dusty bottle out to you,
glad, he said, to give it away
to someone who appreciated
its value and spirit, the years
it took to settle into its richness
and worth. I'm watching again,
each cell alive, as you reach
for the wine, your forearm exposed
below the rolled sleeve, the fine hairs
that sweep along the muscle, glowing,
lifting a little in the afternoon breeze.
I'm memorizing the shape of the moment:
your hand and the small bones
lengthening beneath the skin
as it tightens in the gripping,
in the receiving of the gift, the exact
texture and color of your skin,
and the old man's face, reduced
to its essence. That,
and the brief second
when both of you had a hand on the bottle —
the thing not yet given,
not yet taken, but held
between you, stoppered, full.
And my body is flooded again
with an elemental joy,
holding onto it against another day
in the unknowable future when I'm given

terrible news, some dark burden
I'll be forced to carry. I know
this is useless, and can't possibly work,
but I'm saving that moment, for balance.

SMALL GODS

For My Daughter Who Loves Animals

Once a week, whether the money is there
or not, I write a check for her lessons.
But today, as I waited in the car for her
to finish her chores, after she had wrapped
this one's delicate legs, brushed burrs
and caked mud from that one's tail,
I saw her stop and offer her body
to a horse's itchy head. One arm up,
she gave him the whole length of her side.
And he knew the gesture, understood
the gift, stepped in close on oiled hooves
and pressed his head to her ribcage.
From hip to armpit he raked her body until,
to keep from falling, she leaned into him
full weight, her foot braced
against a tack post for balance.
Before horses, it was snakes, coiled
around her arms like African bracelets.
And before that, stray dogs, cats
of every color, even the misfits,
the abandoned and abused.
It took me so long to learn how to love,
how to give myself up and over to another.
Now I see how she has always
loved them all, snails and spiders,
from the very beginning, without fear or shame,
saw even the least of them, ants,
gnats, heard and answered
even the slightest of their calls.

Planning the Future

I never dreamed my daughter would be 16
until the day arrived with a car full of kids
and balloons, take-out Mexican food
and a Baskin Robbins ice cream cake.
A few months later and she has a boyfriend
in a baseball cap and baggy pants, two gold hoop
earrings and a shaved head. They are happy.
After school they do their homework together,
stretched out on her bed, the door open
to the edge of the legal limit.
Every history question finished deserves
a kiss. They're embarrassed by the names
they've invented for each other,
by their tenderness. Toward evening
they watch MTV, mute the volume
during the commercials and plan their future —
junior college, then marriage, then kids,
what they'll take with them — his dog,
her rat. I'm happy for them, even knowing
what will happen — the last gift, the last
kiss, her huddled on her bed, blinded
by her own bright pain. And I can see clearly
the day she'll walk away, keys on a ring,
a suitcase banging her legs.
Then the real work of motherhood will begin,
the job of waking into each morning, trusting.

Finding What's Lost

In the middle of the poem my daughter reminds me
that I promised to drive her to the bus stop.
She waits a few beats then calls out the time.
Repeats that I've promised.
I keep the line in my head, repeat it under my breath
as I look for my keys, rummage through my purse,
my jacket pockets. When we're in the car, I search
the floor for a Jack-in-the-Box bag, a ticket stub,
a bridge toll dollar, anything to write on.
I'm still repeating my line when she points
out the window and says "Look, there's the poppy
I told you about," and as I turn the corner I see it,
grown through a crack between the sidewalk and the curb.
We talk about it while I scan driveways for kids
on skateboards and bikes, while the old man who runs
the Rexall locks up for the night and a mangy dog
lifts a frail leg and sprays the side of a tree.
Then we talk about her history essay and her boyfriend,
and she asks again about summer vacation, if we're
going somewhere or just staying home. I say
I don't know and ask what she'd rather do, but by now
we're at the bus stop and she leans over
and, this is so unlike her, brushes her lips
quickly against my cheek. Then, without looking back,
she's out the door, and the line, the poem,
is gone, lost somewhere near 8th and G, hovering
like an orange flower over the gravel street.

Homecoming

At the high school football game, the boys
stroke their new muscles, the girls sweeten their lips
with gloss that smells of bubblegum, candy cane,
or cinnamon. In pleated cheerleader skirts
they walk home with each other, practicing yells,
their long bare legs forming in the dark.
Under the arched field lights a girl
in a velvet prom dress stands near the chainlink,
a cone of roses held between her breasts.
Her lanky father, in a corduroy suit, leans
against the fence. While they talk, she slips a foot
in and out of a new white pump, fingers the weave
of her French braid, the glittering earrings.
They could be a couple on their first date, she,
a little shy, he, trying to impress her
with his casual stance. This is the moment
when she learns what she will love: a warm night,
the feel of nylon between her thighs, the fine hairs
on her arms lifting when a breeze
sifts in through the bleachers, cars
igniting their engines, a man bending over her,
smelling the flowers pressed against her neck.

The Aqueduct

We played there on hot
L.A. summers, kids poking through
the slick algae and bloated
tires, the delicate rafts
of mosquito eggs. Open boxcars
pulled gray squares of sky overhead
as we took apples and crackers
from our pockets and ate, watched
the cursing workers from the can factory
gathering at the silver lunch truck
on the opposite ridge. Sometimes
their dark hands held out
triangles of sandwiches, black bottles
of Coke. They called out to us,
waving us over as we hooted
and shoved a tire through the silt,
the slippery silver pools.
We'd put on a show, daring
slides and jumps, crazy
somersaults down the ungiving
cement sides. Other times
we just sat quiet, eating
together, the sulfur heat rising
so their distant faces
wavered as if under water, as ours,
smaller and dimmer, must have
rippled back — the men and women,
their hammered muscles
swelling the seams of blue uniforms,
us skinny kids in our shorts — them,
filled with something like longing,
and us burning with impatience.

Graffiti

Near the Dayton Avenue signal tower,
below the tracks of the Southern P,
skittish brown birds build nests
in what's left of the trees, repeating
their one stunned note, repeating
their small dun selves.
Near the white lime piles
where factories bury their trash,
boys lug grocery sacks of spray cans
to the wall already crazy with pictures
and painted words: COCK, CUNT, KILL,
so carefully and beautifully made,
and the large, elaborate names: *Skeet.*
Damon. JoJo. Cray. From here
they can feel the train grind by,
pulling its row of open boxcars, the blank sky
punched through each empty door. Here,
in blue jeans and bandannas, among
the discarded car seats, the shriveled
condoms and broken glass, they will scrawl
themselves into infinity. One boy
picks up a can of red paint, sprays over
JoJo's name. It glides on effortlessly.
Three smooth strokes and he's gone.

Twelve

Deep in the canyon, under the red branches
of a manzanita, we turned the pages
slowly, seriously, as if it were a holy text,
just as the summer before we had turned
the dark undersides of rocks to interrupt
the lives of ants, or a black stinkbug
and her hard-backed brood.
And because the boys always came,
even though they weren't invited, we never
said anything, except Brenda who whispered
Turn the page when she thought we'd seen enough.
This went on for weeks one summer, a few of us
meeting at the canyon rim at noon, the glossy
magazine fluttering at the tips of our fingers.
Brenda led the way down, and the others
stumbled after blindly, Martin
always with his little brother
hanging off the pocket of his jeans, a blue
pacifier stuck like candy in his mouth.
Every time he yawned, the wet nipple
fell out into the dirt, and Martin, the good brother,
would pick it up, dust it with the underside
of his shirt, then slip it into his own mouth
and suck it clean. And when the turning
of the pages began, ceremoniously, exposing
thigh after thigh, breast after beautiful,
terrible breast, Martin leaned to one side,
and slid the soft palm of his hand
over his baby brother's eyes.

Matinee

Twelve years old, two silver quarters singing
in the crease of my palm, the marquee
three streets up, the blue neon letters
washed out to the same color as the sky.
What made me turn my head sideways, toward
the quiet house where he stood naked
between the trees, trembling in the shade
of a white-washed duplex, a stranger
looking back at me, holding onto himself
in the sparse light, his eyes opening
and closing, opening and closing.
Why didn't I believe what I saw?
I had seen a man naked before.
I had seen my father undressed, his long white
thighs and the dark scratchy patch between them.
I had seen this, over and over, the pale worm
that grew and bruised up into the air, its
smelly milk, its tiring and slow failing.
I knew what was real and what wasn't.
I knew day from night. And I knew about men,
what they hid beneath their clothes,
so why was I crying? Why was I surprised
to see him there, stroking himself
between the trees? And why was I running?
What was I afraid of? I was twelve. I knew
everything. And it was broad daylight,
wasn't it? That was the sun, wasn't it,
pinned to the sky? I had two quarters in my hand,
I could feel them, the ridges along each rim,
the raised faces pressed into my palm.
There were bright cars and sidewalks
and pale green lawns and the movie theater
a single block away, its glittering brick walls

and mirrored doors. I could see it.
I could be there in another minute
if I could only get across the street,
if I could only keep running. And I could see
the poster in its glassed case. I could read
the names of the actors and the looks
on their faces. One of them was holding
a handful of roses, I remember how they looked—
so red and so real and so close I thought
I could touch them, I was so sure I could
just reach out and take them into my arms.

The Ebony Chickering

My mother cooked with lard she kept
in coffee cans beneath the kitchen sink.
Bean-colored linoleum ticked under her flats
as she wore a path from stove to countertop.
Eggs cracked against the lips of smooth
ceramic bowls she beat muffins in,
boxed cakes and cookie dough.
It was the afternoons she worked toward,
the smell of onions scrubbed from her hands,
when she would fold her flowered apron
and feed it through the sticky refrigerator
handle, adjust the spongy curlers on her head
and wrap a loud Hawaiian scarf into a tired knot
around them as she walked toward her piano,
the one thing my father had given her that she loved.
I can still see each gold letter engraved
on the polished lid she lifted and slid
into the piano's dark body, the hidden hammers
trembling like a muffled word,
the scribbled sheets, her rough hands poised
above the keys as she began her daily practice.
Words like *arpeggio* sparkled through my childhood,
her fingers sliding from the black bar of a sharp
to the white of a common note. "This is Bach,"
she would instruct us, the tail of his name hissing
like a cat. "And Chopin," she said, "was French,
like us," pointing to the sheet music. "Listen.
Don't let the letters fool you. It's best
to always trust your ear."

She played parts of fugues and lost concertos,
played hard as we kicked each other on the couch,
while the meat burned and the wet wash wrinkled

in the basket, played Beethoven as if she understood
the caged world of the deaf, his terrible music
pounding its way through the fence slats
and the screened doors of the cul-de-sac, the yards
where other mothers hung clothes on a wire, bent
to weeds, swept the driveways clean.
Those were the years she taught us how to make
quick easy meals, accept the embarrassment
of a messy house, safety pins and rick-rack
hanging from the hem of her dress.
But I knew the other kids didn't own words
like *fortissimo* and *mordant, treble clef*
and *trill,* or have a mother quite as elegant
as mine when she sat at her piano,
playing like she was famous,
so that when the Sparklets man arrived
to fill our water cooler every week
he would lean against the doorjamb and wait
for her to finish, glossy-eyed
as he listened, secretly touching the tips
of his fingers to the tips of her fingers
as he bowed, and she slipped him the check.

Small Gods

I thought my father was a god,
like all the other fathers down the block, floating
home in their gleaming cars filled with food
and thunder, manna and a terrible noise.
And the mothers were lesser gods, fragile
in their thin robes, their hair
so many multicolored clouds.
And we were small, barely human, huddled
half-naked like puppies on a rug, bathed
in the blue TV light, trying to be good.
We watched them from the corners of our eyes
as they swayed through the house on huge
fearless legs, or sat down slowly
with some large idea and a book.
I could not imagine the immense thoughts
they carried in their heads, their hearts
pumping like heavy machinery.
And maybe this was how it had to be, their silence
a rigid religion, a state of eternal grace
we could never know.
And of the animals I tended through those years,
skinny white mice and shivering birds, dogs
with their browbeaten eyes, the cat
who stared back at me with the glazed green irises
of an idiot savant. What did I know
of their terrors, their souls? Like the child I was,
I simply gave them names and fed them.
Day after day, I watched them grow.

Family Reunion

Camera in hand, I call out to them,
one by one, in twos and threes,
working up to the group shots,
the family portrait.
My nephews, scrubbed clean, dressed
in red, hug each other's mirror image
and smile the same smile.
Head to head, their dark hair mingles
as the shutter clicks.
Now I sit the baby between them,
my niece who has my eyes, my nose,
a stranger's wide mouth.
The flash going off in her face
makes her love the small black box
I hold, so much, she is willing to pose
forever, as if I held the force
of the sun, a gorgeous toy, and all
her days balanced in my hands.
Grandmother squeezes in, holds
her baby's babies in her diminishing lap,
circles the shoulders of her son,
her daughters, my own shy daughter,
and pulls them into the frame,
the fine lines of noses and chins
a painter's signature stroke.
I take picture after picture,
the windows going darker
with each bright flash, each face
held up to the repetition of light.
But when I look to see how many frames
are left, I find the tiny window
in the camera is empty, remember
the film left on my dresser

500 miles away. I smile at my family,
ask them to stay where they are
just a few minutes longer as I press
the blank shutter again
and again, burning their images into my own
incorruptible lens, picture
after perfect picture, saving them all
with my naked eye, my bare hands,
the purest light of my love.

Each Sound

Beginnings are brutal, like this accident
of stars colliding, mute explosions
of colorful gases, the mist and dust
that would become our bodies
hurling through black holes, rising,
muck ridden, from pits of tar and clay.
Back then it was easy to have teeth,
claw our way into the trees — it was
accepted, the monkeys loved us, sat
on their red asses clapping and laughing.
We've forgotten the luxury of dumbness,
how once we crouched naked on an outcrop
of rock, the moon huge and untouched
above us, speechless. Now we talk
about everything, incessantly,
our moans and grunts turned on a spit
into warm vowels and elegant consonants.
We say *plethora, demitasse, ozone* and *love*.
We think we know what each sound means.
There are times when something so joyous
or so horrible happens our only response
is an intake of breath, and then
we're back at the truth of it,
that ball of life expanding
and exploding on impact, our heads,
our chests, filled with that first
unspeakable light.

AS IT IS

As It Is

The man I love hates technology, hates
that he's forced to use it: telephones
and microfilm, air conditioning,
car radios and the occasional fax.
He wishes he lived in the old world,
sitting on a stump carving a clothespin
or a spoon. He wants to go back, slip
like lint into his great-great-grandfather's
pocket, reborn as a pilgrim, a peasant,
a dirt farmer hoeing his uneven rows.
He walks when he can, through the hills
behind his house, his dogs panting beside him
like small steam engines. He's delighted
by the sun's slow and simple
descent, the complicated machinery
of his own body. I would have loved him
in any era, in any dark age; I would take him
into the twilight and unwind him, slide
my fingers through his hair and pull him
to his knees. As it is, this afternoon, late
in the twentieth century, I sit on a chair
in the kitchen with my keys in my lap, pressing
the black button on the answering machine
over and over, listening to his message,
his voice strung along the wires outside my window
where the birds balance themselves
and stare off into the trees, thinking
even in the farthest future, in the most
distant universe, I would have recognized
this voice, refracted, as it would be, like light
from some small, uncharted star.

Fast Gas

for Richard

Before the days of self service,
when you never had to pump your own gas,
I was the one who did it for you, the girl
who stepped out at the sound of a bell
with a blue rag in my hand, my hair pulled back
in a straight, unlovely ponytail.
This was before automatic shut-offs
and vapor seals, and once, while filling a tank,
I hit a bubble of trapped air and the gas
backed up, came arcing out of the hole
in a bright gold wave and soaked me — face, breasts,
belly and legs. And I had to hurry
back to the booth, the small employee bathroom
with the broken lock, to change my uniform,
peel the gas-soaked cloth from my skin
and wash myself in the sink.
Light-headed, scrubbed raw, I felt
pure and amazed — the way the amber gas
glazed my flesh, the searing,
subterranean pain of it, how my skin
shimmered and ached, glowed
like rainbowed oil on the pavement.
I was twenty. In a few weeks I would fall,
for the first time, in love, that man waiting
patiently in my future like a red leaf
on the sidewalk, the kind of beauty
that asks to be noticed. How was I to know
it would begin this way: every cell of my body
burning with a dangerous beauty, the air around me
a nimbus of light that would carry me
through the days, how when he found me,

weeks later, he would find me like that,
an ordinary woman who could rise
in flame, all he would have to do
is come close and touch me.

The Thief

What is it when your man sits on the floor
in sweatpants, his latest project
set out in front of him like a small world, maps
and photographs, diagrams and plans, everything
he hopes to build, invent or create,
and you believe in him as you always have,
even after the failures, even more now
as you set your coffee down
and move toward him, to where he sits
oblivious of you, concentrating
in a square of sun —
you step over the rulers and blue graph-paper
to squat behind him, and he barely notices,
though you're still in your robe
which falls open a little as you reach
around his chest, feel for the pink
wheel of each nipple, the slow beat
of his heart, your ear pressed to his back
to listen — and you are torn,
not wanting to interrupt his work
but unable to keep your fingers
from dipping into the ditch in his pants,
torn again with tenderness
for the way his flesh grows unwillingly
toward your curved palm, toward the light,
as if you had planted it, this sweet root,
your mouth already an echo of its shape —
you slip your tongue into his ear
and he hears you, calling him away
from his work, the angled lines of his thoughts,
into the shapeless place you are bound
to take him, over bridges of bone, beyond
borders of skin, climbing over him

into the world of the body, its labyrinth
of ladders and stairs — and you love him
like the first time you loved him,
with equal measures of expectancy
and fear and awe, taking him with you
into the soft geometry of the flesh, the earth
before its sidewalks and cities,
its glistening spires,
stealing him back from the world he loves
into this other world he cannot build without you.

Landrum's Diner, Reno

We slouch, half-asleep on Christmas Day,
in a domed metal diner with seven red stools.
Three lone men drink coffee, glass shakers
of salt, pepper and sugar between them,
a pyramid of creamers. A young family
orders breakfast. They taste
from each other's plates as the sun
leaks through the windows, spilling onto
their heads, their hands, like butter.
After seven years, we have begun
to love each other, to trust
the small favors, the daily gifts.
Not that there isn't passion: the hotel bed
left a mess, bright wrappers and ribbons
scattered across the floor. But we love
where we've come to, this drowsy morning
among strangers, slumped shoulder to shoulder,
holding each other up. Our round and clumsy
waitress owns the place, trundles
between the counters filling cup after cup.
When she walks the short length of the diner,
each floorboard aches under her weight, shakes
us awake. She stops before us and lowers
her face, unlined, moon-shaped,
between our faces, her hands outstretched
palms up, in love with her work, asking
what more we could want?

Sunday Radio

From my husband's window I hear a woman
singing, low in her throat, a song meant to break

a thousand hearts into bloom.
In his loneliness he sings too,

losing words and notes along the way
but staying with her, sure of the refrain.

This is the hardest part of the marriage: knowing.
Clipping the roses, knowing. Raking the leaves.

Pausing at the staircase to listen
to how his voice breaks, then goes on with the song.

Enough Music

Sometimes, when we're on a long drive,
and we've talked enough and listened
to enough music and stopped twice,
once to eat, once to see the view,
we fall into this rhythm of silence.
It swings back and forth between us
like a rope over a lake.
Maybe it's what we don't say
that saves us.

Kaleidoscope

I remember sex before my husband
as a vague, vagrant landscape
of taller, darker men, all thick hair
and hands, the full lips of the rich past.
And sometimes, when I'm taking a sidewalk
full tilt, my heels chipping
the glittering cement, I feel their eyes,
their sweet lost fingers
tugging at my clothes — the one
who fell behind just to watch me walk,
to see me as a stranger might,
then caught up to catch
a handful of my hair, turn me around,
pull me back into his body's deep folds.
They all come back, tenacious
as angels, to lean against me
at the movies, the beach — a shoulder
or a thigh pressed to mine, lashes
black and matted, and always
naked, clean and pure as souls slipped
glistening from the body's warm wick,
like my husband's fingers when he dips
into me, then lifts them
to his face, heavy with glaze, the leaves
crowded against our window, shivering.

This Close

In the room where we lie, light
stains the drawn shades yellow.
We sweat and pull at each other, climb
with our fingers the slippery ladders of rib.
Wherever our bodies touch, the flesh
comes alive. Heat and need, like invisible
animals, gnaw at my breasts, the soft
insides of your thighs. What I want
I simply reach out and take, no delicacy now,
the dark human bread I eat handful
by greedy handful. Eyes, fingers, mouths,
sweet leeches of desire. Crazy woman,
her brain full of bees, see how her palms curl
into fists and beat the pillow senseless.
And when my body finally gives in to it
then pulls itself away, salt-laced
and arched with its final ache, I am
so grateful I would give you anything, anything.
If I loved you, being this close would kill me.

Afterwards

when we sat side by side
on the edge of the unmade bed,
staring blindly at our knees, our feet,
our clothes stranded in the middle of the floor
like small, crumpled islands,
you put your arm around my shoulder
in that gesture usually reserved
for those of the same sex — equals,
friends, as if we'd
accomplished something together,
like climbing a hill or painting a house,
your hand at rest over the curved bone
of my shoulder, my loud nipples
softening into sleep.
Stripped of our want, our wildness, we sat
naked and tired and companionable
in the sleek silence, innocent
of what we'd said, what we'd done,
our breath slowing, our heads tipped
and touching at the crown,
like a couple of kids
slumped on a dock in the sun, our legs
dangling above the bright water,
admiring each other's reflections.

2 AM

When I came with you that first time
on the floor of your office, the dirty carpet
under my back, the heel of one foot
propped on your shoulder, I went ahead
and screamed, full-throated, as loud
and as long as my body demanded,
because somewhere, in the back of my mind,
packed in the smallest neurons still capable
of thought, I remembered
we were in a warehouse district
and that no sentient being resided for miles.
Afterwards, when I could unclench
my hands and open my eyes, I looked up.
You were on your knees, your arms
stranded at your sides, so still —
the light from the crooknecked lamp
sculpting each lift and delicate twist,
the lax muscles, the smallest veins
on the backs of your hands. I saw
the ridge of each rib, the blue hollow
pulsing at your throat, all the colors
in your long blunt cut hair which hung
over your face like a raffia curtain
in some south sea island hut.
And as each bright synapse unfurled
and followed its path, I recalled
a story I'd read that explained why women
cry out when they come — that it's
the call of the conqueror, a siren howl
of possession. So I looked again
and it felt true, your whole body
seemed defeated, owned, having taken on
the aspect of a slave in shackles, the wrists

loosely bound with invisible rope.
And when you finally spoke you didn't
lift your head but simply moaned the word *god*
on an exhalation of breath — I knew then
I must be merciful, benevolent,
impossibly kind.

The Lovers

She is about to come. This time,
they are sitting up, joined below the belly,
feet cupped like sleek hands praying
at the base of each other's spines.
And when something lifts within her
toward a light she's sure, once again,
she can't bear, she opens her eyes
and sees his face is turned away,
one arm behind him, hand splayed
palm down on the mattress, to brace himself
so he can lever his hips, touch
with the bright tip the innermost spot.
And she finds she *can't* bear it —
not his beautiful neck, stretched and corded,
not his hair fallen to one side like beach grass,
not the curved wing of his ear, washed thin
with daylight, deep pink of the inner body.
What she can't bear is that she can't see his face,
not that she thinks this exactly — she is rocking
and breathing — it's more her body's thought,
opening, as it is, into its own sheer truth.
So that when her hand lifts of its own volition
and slaps him, twice on the chest,
on that pad of muscled flesh just above the nipple,
slaps him twice, fast, like a nursing child
trying to get a mother's attention,
she's startled by the sound,
though when he turns his face to hers —
which is what her body wants, his eyes
pulled open, as if she had bitten —
she does reach out and bite him, on the shoulder,
not hard, but with the power infants have
over those who have borne them, tied as they are

to the body, and so, tied to the pleasure,
the exquisite pain of this world.
And when she lifts her face he sees
where she's gone, knows she can't speak,
is traveling toward something essential,
toward the core of her need, so he simply
watches, steadily, with an animal calm
as she arches and screams, watches the face that,
if she could see it, she would never let him see.

Kissing

They are kissing, on a park bench,
on the edge of an old bed, in a doorway
or on the floor of a church. Kissing
as the streets fill with balloons
or soldiers, locusts or confetti, water
or fire or dust. Kissing down through
the centuries under sun or stars, a dead tree,
an umbrella, amid derelicts. Kissing
as Christ carries his cross, as Gandhi
sings his speeches, as a bullet
careens through the air toward a child's
good heart. They are kissing,
long, deep, spacious kisses, exploring
the silence of the tongue, the mute
rungs of the upper palate, hungry
for the living flesh. They are still
kissing when the cars crash and the bombs
drop, when the babies are born crying
into the white air, when Mozart bends
to his bowl of soup and Stalin
bends to his garden. They are kissing
to begin the world again. Nothing
can stop them. They kiss until their lips
swell, their thick tongues quickening
to the budded touch, licking up
the sweet juices. I want to believe
they are kissing to save the world,
but they're not. All they know
is this press and need, these two-legged
beasts, their faces like roses crushed
together and opening, they are covering
their teeth, they are doing what they have to do
to survive the worst, they are sealing

the hard words in, they are dying
for our sins. In a broken world they are
practicing this simple and singular act
to perfection. They are holding
onto each other. They are kissing.

Acknowledgments

Grateful acknowledgment is made to the editors of the following journals and anthologies in which some of these poems or earlier versions of them first appeared:

Agni: "Dust"
American Poetry Review: "The Thief," "The Lovers," "Sunday Radio," and "What Could Happen"
American Voice: "Aphasia" and "Late October"
Bakunin: "The Aqueduct" and "Kaleidoscope"
Haight Ashbury Literary Journal: "Enough Music" and "Singing Back the World"
New England Review: "The Job"
Tar River Poetry: "Homecoming" and "Landrum's Diner, Reno"
Yellow Silk: "Twelve," "This Close," "Fast Gas," and "For My Daughter Who Loves Animals"
ZYZZYVA: "After Twelve Days of Rain," "Finding What's Lost," and "What We Carry"

"This Close" was included in *Lovers* (The Crossing Press, 1992); "The Thief" and "The Lovers" were included in *Wild Nights* (Shambala Publications, 1994).

My special thanks to the Heart's Desire Poetry Gang: Christina, Laurie and Ron, and especially Kim, who sings when I can't, the two Janes, Judy, Geri, the two Mollys, Jeanne, Joyce, the two Steves and V, Brenda, Patricia, Stefanie and Sam, Kathy and Tom: the Cosmic Travelers, Lily, Donald, Leslie and Howard, Chana, who I didn't thank enough the last time, Mills College, Oliver's Books, my family, who have entrusted me with their stories, the BOA Boys, Don Schenker and the heaven of Hurd's Gulch, Tristem and Christopher, my students, my teachers, Rosen, my mentor and healer, Phil, who keeps on noticing, Boo and Daphne, and to Al, for every little thing he does.

About the Author

Dorianne Laux was born in 1952 in Augusta, Maine, and raised in Southern California. Between the ages of 18 and 30 she worked as a gas station manager, sanatorium cook, maid, and donut holer. A single mother, she took occasional classes and poetry workshops at the local junior college, writing poems during shift breaks. In 1983 she moved to Berkeley, California, where she began writing in earnest. Supported by scholarships and grants, she returned to school when her daughter Tristem was 9, and was graduated with honors from Mills College in the Spring of 1988 with a B.A. Degree in English. Her first book, *Awake*, with an introduction by Philip Levine, was published in 1990 and nominated for the Bay Area Book Reviewers Award. In the same year she was awarded a Fellowship in Poetry from the National Endowment for the Arts. She now lives in Petaluma, California, where she teaches private poetry workshops. In the Fall of 1994 she will move to Eugene, Oregon, to join the faculty at the University of Oregon's Program in Creative Writing. *What We Carry* is her second book of poems.

BOA EDITIONS, LTD.
AMERICAN POETS CONTINUUM SERIES

Printed in the USA
CPSIA information can be obtained
at www.ICGtesting.com
JSHW082226140824
68134JS00015B/747

9 781880 238073